DISCARDED

To foster a young child's love for reading, one must begin by choosing quality read-aloud books about topics the child is interested in. One must then look for opportunities to bring the story, characters, artwork, concepts and ideas off of the page and put it into the hands of the child. *Exploring Books through Play* will take you on a journey through ten fabulous children's books. Along the way, you will be inspired by the beautiful photos, creative processes, and the thoughtful ideas each contributing author shares to help expand and nurture your child's love for literacy.

Deborah Stewart, M.Ed
founder of *Teach* Preschool, teacher and
author of *Ready for Kindergarten!*

Books can act as both windows and mirrors for children. They can shine a light on experiences that are unfamiliar and uncomfortable as much as they can make that unusual child feel as though they are no longer alone. The authors of this book help parents and educators tap into that potential to use these amazing vehicles for learning to teach more than just literacy and numeracy skills.

Allison McDonald, B.Ed
founder of *No Time for Flashcards,* teacher
and author of *Raising a Rock-Star Reader*

Great children's books help kids discover more about themselves and others. *Exploring Books Through Play* utilizes those wonderful books through playful and engaging activities taking kids deeper into learning about themselves and their world. Each activity can stand alone or build upon each other to create a rich experience for our kids and their journey of becoming accepting and loving individuals.

Jodie Rodriguez, MA and MEA
founder of *Growing Book by Book,* former
principal, reading specialist and curriculum
coordinator

exploring books through play

50 activities based on books about
friendship, acceptance & empathy

Colleen Beck, OTR/L, Jen Kossowan, B.Ed,
Chelsey Marashian, B.Ed,
Meredith Magee Donnelly, MS, Ed & Jaime Williams

ISBN-13:9780692758144
ISBN-10: 0692758143

Printed in the United States of America.

Library of Congress Control Number: 2016912143
Meredith Magee Donnelly, West Hartford, CT

Photography by Colleen Beck, Jen Kossowan, Chelsey Marashian,
Meredith Magee Donnelly and Jaime Williams.

Cover design by Meredith Magee Donnelly.

To Quinn, Luca, Charlotte, Dave, Mom & Dad -MMD

To my Buggy and Buddy- Lucy & Theo- CM

With all of my love to my Lillian, Jackson, Julia, and Emily -CB

To my boys- JW

To my bubbas, Gracen & Sam -JK

contents

contents

contents

introduction

Two years ago a group of bloggers joined together for a series entitled Preschool Book Club. The series utilized children's literature as inspiration for play-based activities focusing on art, literacy, science, mathematics, sensory exploration, gross motor development and fine motor skills. That 5 week series was such a success that it continued to grow.

Exploring Books Through Play: Friendship, Acceptance and Empathy is the beginning of a new journey into print. Focusing on high quality children's literature centered on friendship, acceptance and empathy, this book is designed to be used in home and school settings and is perfect for large or small groups. This book is ideal for children ages 3-8 years old as the activities can be adapted for multiple skill levels and developmental stages.

The book is a celebration of play-based learning. As you work through the activities in the book, children will naturally be discussing the characters, delving deeper into the lessons, bringing the stories to life and falling further in love with literature.

how to use the book

Always begin by reading the children's books and having a discussion. Pose open-ended questions that focus on how the characters are feeling, reasons why they may have acted in a certain way, what children would do the same and what they might do differently. Each book's activities can be used on their own and do not need to be followed in any particular order. The activities can be explored in isolation or as small group choice time centers. As the children play, follow up with conversations centered on friendship, empathy and acceptance. Use each group of activities as a starting point for inspiration to create more playful opportunities.

A Sick Day for Amos McGee
by Philip C. Stead

Caring for friends is one of the most important things a person can do. As a zookeeper Amos McGee shows each animal the individual love and care they deserve. When Amos wakes up with a cold the zoo animals hop a bus to care for their friend.

happy thoughts letters

Meredith Magee Donnelly, MS, Ed - Homegrown Friends

The first time I read *A Sick Day for Amos McGee* I fell in love. From the breathtaking pencil and watercolor illustrations to the heart-warming friendships, I knew we needed to read this book over and over again. This activity helps children focus on thinking of others while exploring the way the illustrations were created in the book.

materials

watercolor paper
liquid watercolors
paint brushes
pencil
marker (optional)

Begin by reading the book and exploring the different ways the characters care for each other. Introduce the idea that one way we can show we care for each other is by sending a happy letter.

Using pieces of watercolor paper folded in half begin by drawing pictures using pencils. Pose the question *What type of pictures would make a person happy? Who do you want to send a letter to?* Maybe there is a family or friend who could use some happy mail or a class could send letters to a local children's hospital.

After drawing the pictures use watercolor paints to color the different sections of the pictures.

Mail the letters knowing you will brighten someone's day!

pretend play care center

Jen Kossowan, B.Ed – Mama.Papa.Bubba.

A Sick Day for Amos McGee is the perfect book for encouraging kindness, caring and helping friends - things that we as parents and teachers do our very best to foster within our kids. In this dramatic play activity, children will have the opportunity to care for sick friends and practice putting the needs of others in front of their own.

materials

pillows,
warm blankets
stuffed animals
picture books
fuzzy socks
cup and tea bag
bowl and spoon
empty medicine bottle
washcloths

Set up your pretend play care center in a cozy corner, making sure that all of the supplies are organized, inviting and easily accessible.

Begin by reading the book and discussing how you can help someone when he or she is feeling ill. Pose the questions *How do you feel when you're not well?* and *What makes you feel better?* Encourage the children to share their answers.

Invite the children over to the care center to explore. Ask them about what they see and how they think the items might be useful when a friend is sick.

Encourage the children to take turns being the person who is feeling ill and being the friends who are there to help. The helpers can fix their sick friend a cup of tea, make sure he is comfortable and warm, whip him up a bowl of noodle soup, give him a dose of medicine, or fold up a cool washcloth for his forehead. Role play is a powerful tool and there's really no right or wrong way to play!

patchwork paper quilt

Chelsey Marashian, B.Ed – Buggy and Buddy

A Sick Day for Amos McGee is a great story for opening up a discussion about showing empathy for others, especially when they aren't feeling well. The kids and I use this story to focus on helping family members feel better when they are sick. One of the ways we help each other is by making them comfortable while they are recovering (like letting them snuggle with a special blanket).

materials

sheet of construction paper
patterned paper (like scrapbooking paper) and/or solid paper cut into squares
glue stick
optional: yarn

In this activity, children will create a paper quilt to keep someone cozy while they are feeling ill. You can also use this quilt project to practice math skills like patterning, spatial awareness, and shape recognition.

Cut some scrapbooking paper into squares. (You can also use fabric scraps in place of the scrapbooking paper.) Use the squares to create a design on your full sheet of construction paper and glue them in place with your glue stick. Younger children can describe the shapes and patterns they see on the paper as they glue. Older children might want to create an actual quilt design using their paper squares.

Once your sheet of paper is covered with squares, you've finished your paper quilt. You can personalize it any way you would like. We added a face peeking out of one of our paper quilts. It would also make a nice cover for a get well card.

chai tea playdough

Jaime Williams – Frogs, Snails and Puppy Dog Tails

What a wonderful story of friendship. The kids and I love the tea time part in the book and they can never get enough pretend play in their play kitchen making coffee and tea. The chai tea playdough is a fun sensory experience. This no-cook recipe is so easy and can be made without a stove making it perfect for a classroom. It smells amazing.

materials

flour
salt
oil
water
chai tea
pretend play tea cups and pot

Begin by making the chai tea playdough. With the children's help add 2 cups of flour, 1 cup of salt and 1 teaspoon of olive oil. Then add 1 cup of water. Mix the ingredients with hands or spoon and then cut a few tea bags open and pour them into the bowl of playdough. Mix together.

Set up the playdough with tea cups, a tea pot, plates, a tray and the tags from the tea bags. Children will enjoy pretending to add playdough to the tea cups, asking friends if it is sweet enough or too hot. Children can explore the smell and texture of the playdough making this a fun sensory activity.

Store the chai playdough in a plastic storage bag for future use.

red balloon suncatcher

Colleen Beck, OTR/L – Sugar Aunts

Amos knows that friends come in many shapes and sizes. He shares his time and kindness with his friends at the zoo, and when Amos himself needs encouragement, his many species of friends return the favor. Pencil illustrations with spots of color tell as much of the story as the words do. This balloon suncatcher can fill windows and remind us to encourage friends with a smile or a bright spot of encouragement no matter where we go.

materials

black cardstock
clear contact paper
red tissue paper, cut into squares
black yarn
glue
photograph of each child as if they are holding a balloon
tape

To make this balloon suncatcher, you will need to prepare two items in advance: The photograph of the child should be taken as if the child is holding a balloon. The black string also needs to be created a day in advance. To make the black string of the balloon, cut a length of black yarn. Saturate the yarn in glue and position it in a wavy line on wax paper. Allow the string to dry overnight.

To make the balloon: Gently fold the black cardstock in half. (Don't crease the paper.) From the folded side, cut half of a balloon shape, with an inner circle cut out as well. Lay the balloon shape flat on a table surface, smoothing the fold at the center. Remove the backing from the contact paper and carefully place it on the table, sticky side up. Place the balloon on the contact paper.

Position the red tissue paper squares on the contact paper inside the balloon shape, making sure all areas of the contact paper are covered with tissue paper. Peel the black yarn from the wax paper and tape it to the back of the balloon and the back of the photograph.

Hang the balloon suncatcher in a window and enjoy the bright color shining through.

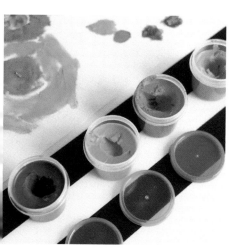

The Day the Crayons Quit
by Drew Daywalt

One day Duncan opens his crayon box and finds a surprise. All the crayons are gone and have left letters for him describing what is bothering them. Duncan listens to his crayon friends and responds in the most beautiful way.

crayon box craft

Chelsey Marashian, B.Ed – Buggy and Buddy

This activity is inspired by the notes the crayons leave explaining their feelings and complaints as to why they have quit. Because this book is a great way to encourage focusing on another point of view, I decided to create a project that allows children to illustrate what their own crayons would say if they were to quit just like the ones in the story.

materials

empty crayon box
tape
scissors
pen or pencil
crayon and word bubble printable (page 132)

Talk about the feelings each crayon had in the story. As you go through each crayon, write what you'd like each crayon to say inside a word bubble on the printable. You can either have children choose something that was said in the actual book to practice retelling, or let them come up with their own sentences the crayons might say. Children that are not yet writing can dictate to an adult what they would like written in their word bubbles.

Cut out the word bubbles and crayons. Tape the word bubbles to their corresponding crayons.

Tape the crayons and word bubbles onto your crayon box.

Display your finished project.

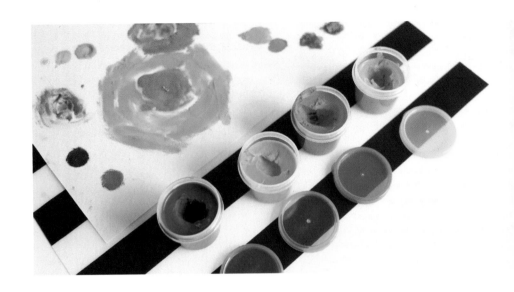

crayon finger paint

Jen Kossowan, B.Ed – Mama.Papa.Bubba.

If you're a parent, teacher, or caregiver, you most likely have old, tired crayons that really want to quit. In this hands-on science and art activity, children will have the opportunity to turn their broken crayon bits into unique finger paints before using them to create some beautiful, original artwork.

materials

old broken crayons
coconut oil
tin or silicone baking cups
wooden popsicle sticks
small containers with lids
card stock or watercolor paper

Begin by reading the book and discussing some of the reasons Duncan's crayons have quit (they're old, tired, tiny, poorly cared for, etc.). Together, brainstorm ways that old, broken crayons can be put to good use. If it's not mentioned, introduce the fact that they can be used to make a brand new art supply... finger paint!

To create the paint, invite the children to sort the broken crayons into groups of similar colors before breaking them into small pieces. Transfer each color group into baking cups and add just slightly less coconut oil than you have wax crayon. Next, place the cups on a baking sheet and pop it into an oven warmed to 250 degrees F. This is a great time to turn the oven light on and ask the children to predict what might happen.

As the crayons and coconut oil melt, take the paints out once or twice and give them a good stir with the wooden sticks. When they're fully melted, transfer the paints into small containers and let them harden.

Invite the children to create an original piece of artwork. The paints will have a thick, paste-like texture and work best when slightly warm, so placing them somewhere sunny a few minutes before using them is helpful. The heat and friction from little fingers also helps them to blend beautifully. Have the children title their finished pieces and sign them.

paper doll crayons

Jaime Williams – Frogs, Snails and Puppy Dog Tails

This activity is inspired by children wanting to dress the "naked" Peach crayon. Children love that part of the story. These paper doll crayons are a perfect tool for children to play with while reading the book.

materials

paper crayons (page 133)
printable clothes (page 134 & 135)
laminator
scissors
velcro dots
download crayon clothes

Prior to introducing the activity print, cut out and laminate the crayons and clothes. Cut out the crayons and clothes. Add the small Velcro dots to the crayons and clothes. This allows the children to play with these paper doll crayons over and over again.

Children can explore the different names of clothing, colors and use the crayons as a counting tool.

The paper doll crayons can be used as a prop while reading the story and revisited after the story as well as a table top activity. This is such a fun way for children to explore the book again and again.

dear crayon activity

Meredith Magee Donnelly, MS, Ed – Homegrown Friends

The crayons in Duncan's box feel underappreciated and overworked. Sometimes we forget to tell the people and things in our lives how much we truly care for them. Children will take the time to pick their favorite crayons and write a letter to them telling them why they are their favorites.

materials

1 copy per child Dear Crayon writing sheet (page 136)
crayons
pencils

After reading the book focus the discussion on *Why do you think the crayons felt the need to write the letters? Why did they not want to color anymore?* Talk about how we need to take the time to feel grateful for the people and things in our lives. Introduce the idea of writing to our favorite crayons sharing why we think they are great.

Give each child a writing sheet and have them pick a crayon they will write to. Children can write independently or dictate the words and have an adult write.

Once they finish writing, give children a piece of white paper to draw a picture using their favorite crayons.

crayon shaving shapes

Colleen Beck, OTR/L – Sugar Aunts

The crayons want a break from coloring, so why not use them in a creative, no-mess, sensory activity? This sensory shape bag uses many colors from the crayon box and adds a sensory twist to learning. Practice math concepts such as shape identification with a fine motor component as children trace shapes with their finger.

materials

4-5 crayons
hand-held pencil sharpener
plastic sandwich bag
permanent marker
tape
1 cup clear shampoo or body lotion

Use the hand-held pencil sharpener to sharpen the crayons, collecting the shavings. On the plastic sandwich bag, draw shapes with the permanent marker. Colored markers can be used, but black works best for seeing the shapes once the sensory bag is filled.

Pour the shampoo into the plastic bag and add the crayon shavings. Seal the baggie (glue can be added to strengthen the opening) and fold over the top edge. Tape the opening down before allowing children to play with the sensory bag.

Show the kids how to work the crayon shavings into the shape outlines, using their fingers.

Leonardo the Terrible Monster
By Mo Willems

Leonardo thinks he is a terrible monster because he cannot scare anyone no matter how hard he tries. When he finally does learn to scare a little boy, he learns it doesn't feel very good. He has an important decision to make.

monster mirror craft

Chelsey Marashian, B.Ed – Buggy and Buddy

Not only does *Leonardo the Terrible Monster* lend itself to exploring the different feelings people can have. In this activity children will create their very own mirrors and use them to practice making different faces based on various emotions. This is a great way for children to learn to read social cues and develop empathy for others.

materials

thick cardboard
paint and paintbrush
scissors
mylar sheet (or other reflective material)
glue
construction paper or cardstock
markers

Start by making your mirror craft. Draw and cut out a mirror shape from a thick piece of cardboard.

Decide how you want to decorate your mirror. We designed ours to resemble the monsters from the story, but children can make mirrors with various designs or even mirrors that resemble themselves!

Paint your mirror any color you'd like, and let it dry. Cut out a piece of mylar sheeting that fits inside your mirror shape and glue it in place. Use construction paper and markers to add any details to your mirror. We made horns, ears, and even a hat and glued them right on our mirror.

Reread the story and talk about the different emotions the characters display during the book. *What clues do you see that let you know how they're feeling?* Practice making different feeling faces in your mirror just like the characters. *What other feelings do people have? Can you show that feeling in your mirror?*

Save your mirror for practicing more feeling faces later on or to use in imaginative play.

slime monsters

Meredith Magee Donnelly, MS, Ed – Homegrown Friends

Leonardo learns that it is much more fun to be friendly than to be scary. After reading the book kids can continue having fun by making their own friendly slime monsters. And maybe a few scary ones too!

materials

ingredients for slime:
borax
water
white glue
liquid watercolors or food coloring
accessories such as googly eyes, stones, plastic gems

Prior to introducing the slime monsters, make the slime. In one bowl mix 1/2 cup water with 1 teaspoon borax. In another bowl mix 1 cup of glue with 1 cup of warm water, plus liquid watercolor or food coloring. Slowly add the borax mixture to the glue mixture a little bit at a time. As you stir, the slime will begin to form. Keep adding the borax mixture and knead with your hands until the slime is fully formed. Pour out any additional liquid. Optional: repeat the process for additional colors.

Give each child a small amount of slime and access to the various accessories. Explain to the children that they can use the accessories to make all different types of monsters. *What would a friendly monster look like? What would a scary monster or a silly monster look like?*

friend bean bag toss

Colleen Beck, OTR/L – Sugar Aunts

This gross motor bean bag toss activity helps children realize what it means to be a good friend. Kids toss bean bags onto unique monster faces while discovering the many qualities of friendship. Leonardo's determination to be a terrible monster will match the determination of children as they build gross motor skills in a creative bean bag toss. Kids will love to play in a group of friends with this bean bag monster activity.

materials

coffee filters
paint
plastic forks
construction paper
glue
markers
bean bags

Spread the coffee filters out on a table. Use forks to paint the coffee filters, creating fur-like textured art. Paint colors can be combined to create colorful monster faces on the coffee filters. Add details like eyes, noses, horns, teeth, and mouths using the construction paper, marker, and glue. Allow the coffee filter monsters to dry overnight.

To play with these monster faces, spread them out on the floor or grass. Provide the children with bean bags and ask them to try to toss the bean bags onto each monster face. When the bean bag lands on a monster, the children should call out qualities of a good friend. Children can explore concepts such as encouragement, sharing, and taking turns as they play in a group.

paper bag monsters

Jaime Williams – Frogs, Snails and Puppy Dog Tails

The children just loved this book and had me read it more than once. Once the children had gotten their fill of reading the story over and over, it was time for a fun book-inspired craft. Finding fun and easy ways to extend a book through crafts and activities is always a hit with my children. The paper bag puppets are perfect for playtime or as a prop when reading the story.

materials

brown paper bag
pink construction paper
white cardstock or thick paper
glue
blue buttons
brown permanent marker

Prior to introducing the activity, gather the craft supplies. To create a Leonardo puppet, begin by tracing pink noses like Leonardo's on construction paper. Use a brown permanent marker to make nostrils. Trace horns on white cardstock paper. Cardstock works well because it is a thick paper. Blue buttons work well for eyes.

Children can glue on the white horns, the pink nose and two blue buttons for eyes. Once the children finish, draw eyebrows and a mouth. Now each child has his own Leonardo monster.

The great thing about the paper bag monster puppets is that children can use their imaginations if they want to create their own unique monster. Either way, it is a fun book inspired activity to go with this darling story of a monster who figures out what he wants to be.

wooden spoon puppets

Jen Kossowan, B.Ed – Mama.Papa.Bubba.

In true Mo Willems style, *Leonardo the Terrible Monster*'s sparse text conveys a message big in heart, which makes the story absolutely perfect for retelling and guiding dramatic play. In this art and drama activity, children will create a pair of Leonardo and Sam-inspired wooden spoon puppets and use them to retell the story and create story lines of their own.

materials

wooden spoons
acrylic craft paint
paint brushes
felt pieces , googly eyes, yarn , pipe cleaners
scissors
craft glue
permanent markers

Begin by reading the book and discussing the big decision Leonardo made. Ask children to share why they think Leonardo made the choice he did and pose the question *Would you have made the same decision?*

Explain that you'll be creating your own Leonardo and Sam-inspired wooden spoon puppets. Give the children two wooden spoons each and encourage them to think about what they'd like their child and monster friends to look like. Some children may choose to try to replicate Leonardo and Sam, some may create themselves and a monster friend, and some may choose to create a completely original child and monster pair, all of which are perfectly wonderful ways to approach the project.

Invite the children to paint the spoons in their desired colors first, allowing them to dry fully afterwards. Next, with the craft materials set out in divided trays and the craft glue nearby, invite the children to begin adding onto their painted spoons. They may cut out noses from felt, form glasses from pipe cleaners, or add a head of hair using yarn - anything goes!

When the wooden spoons are fully dry, invite the children to put on a puppet show. *Leonardo the Terrible Monster* will likely help shape their narratives, but the children will undoubtedly take their stories in their own directions too.

Boy + Bot
By Ame Dyckman

Boy and Bot have the best time together, but when Bot's power is off, Boy tries all his favorite things to make him feel better. When Boy falls asleep Bot tries to fix him, but no luck. Thankfully, the Inventor helps out and the friends can play again.

playdough robots

Jaime Williams – Frogs, Snails and Puppy Dog Tails

Playdough robots are a wonderful activity for multiple age groups. This makes the exploration perfect for a home or classroom setting. This activity is perfect for encouraging children to use their imaginations to create their own bot friend.

materials

playdough
pipe cleaners
googly eyes
mini clothespins
miscellaneous craft supplies

NOTE: playdough recipe on page 108-109

Set out miscellaneous supplies with the playdough. Homemade playdough or store bought playdough both work well. Keep *Boy + Bot* on the table for inspiration while creating your own bots. Playdough is a great sensory material and perfect for fine motor skills. Kneading, rolling, and molding playdough lets kids work out their tiny hand muscles.

Mold bodies and heads out of playdough for the bots. Children can add googly eyes, clothespins and metal beads for the face. Pipe cleaners come in handy for legs and arms for their bot friends. Once the bots are completed, children can name their new robot friends.

shape robots

Chelsey Marashian, B.Ed – Buggy and Buddy

Boy + Bot is an excellent story for initiating a discussion with children on appreciating each other's differences. We use it as a springboard to discuss how our differences make us unique and can even make friendships extra special. In this activity, not only will kids get the opportunity to express their creativity by making all kinds of interesting and unique robots, but because the robots are made with shapes, they'll get some geometry practice too!

materials

construction paper
graph paper (optional)
scissors
glue
markers or crayons
googly eyes, buttons, or other loose parts

Cut out various shapes from your colored construction paper and place them in a tray or somewhere where your child can easily access them. Invite older children to cut out their own shapes.

Glue the different shapes onto a piece of construction paper or graph paper to make a robot. Add details to your robot using markers, crayons, googly eyes, or other craft materials.

Talk about your different robots you made. *What shapes did you use? How are the different robots alike? How are they different?*

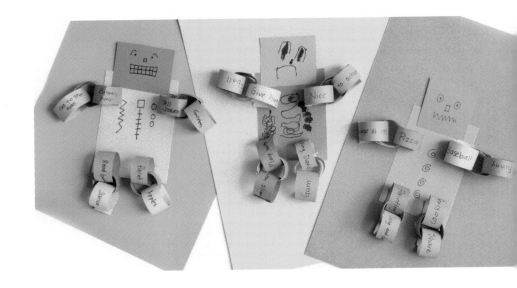

robot character traits

Colleen Beck, OTR/L – Sugar Aunts

Explore individual characteristics and personality traits with this *Boy + Bot* inspired robot craft. Children can identify aspects that make them unique while realizing that we are all so alike yet so different. These colorful robots use chain links to connect traits that make each child who they are. Children can realize that just like Boy and Bot, they can be friends with others who are different than themselves.

materials

colorful cardstock, cut into rectangles, squares, and strips (for the chain links)
glue stick
pen

Have children construct their robots using the large rectangle and square cardstock paper. Ask children to draw features on their robot.

Using the strips of cardstock, children can write or dictate likes, personality traits, and things that make them a great friend to others. Ideas for the chain links might include: favorite foods/sports/ activities, attributes of a good friend, and items that make that child special. After writing details on each chain link piece, glue them together to create the robot's arms and legs.

As children are creating their robots, discuss the concept of caring for and becoming friends with others who are different than themselves. Talk about the idea of one friend who likes a particular food or activity can be friends and care for a friend who likes completely different things.

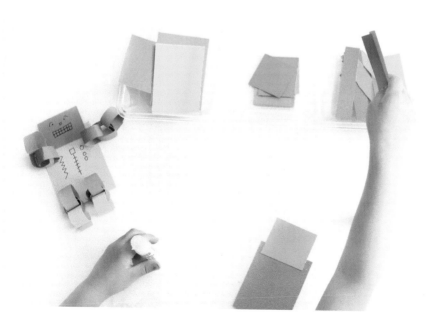

magnetic robots

Jen Kossowan, B.Ed – Mama.Papa.Bubba.

When I first read *Boy + Bot* I immediately fell in love. It's a lovely blend of sweetness and humor, and a perfect depiction of true friendship. In this hands-on activity, children will explore magnetism and use their creativity to construct their very own 'bot' friends.

materials

tin cans, emptied and washed
spray paint (if desired)
googly eyes, buttons, pompoms
button magnets, magnetic marbles, pipe cleaners
nuts and bolts
hot glue
divided tray

Begin with some simple prep work. Spray paint the cans and let dry (optional). Use a hot glue gun to attach button magnets to the googly eyes, buttons, and pompoms before placing all of the loose parts in a divided tray.

Read the story and discuss what makes Boy and Bot special and unique. Discuss *How are they similar?* and *How are they different?* Introduce the fact that you can make your own bot friends by using tin cans and an assortment of magnetic parts.

Set out the materials and invite the children to select a tin can base for their bot. Encourage them to use the parts to create their robot friend, reminding them that the pieces can easily be rearranged as they please.

Invite the children to share their robots. Ask questions such as *Does your friend have a name?* and *What makes him or her unique?* You can keep the bots on display or disassemble them and store the building station for next time.

roll a robot game

Meredith Magee Donnelly, MS, Ed – Homegrown Friends

Children will love a chance to make their own robot friends after reading the book. Race to see who can make their own Bot first with this fun roll a robot game. This game encourages turn-taking, communication, number recognition and using a key to play the game.

materials

roll a robot game sheet (page 137)
robot printable parts (page 138)
die
laminator (optional)

Prior to introducing the game, print out the Roll a Robot Game sheet and copies of the robot parts. Decide how many children will be playing the game at one time (4-6 per group works well) and print a complete set of robot parts per child. Cut out the body parts. If you would like to keep this game long term, I recommend laminating the body parts and cutting them out.

After reading the book introduce the game by explaining that the children will have a chance to make their own Bots. Hand out a complete set of body parts to each child. Next show each side of the die and review that the number of dots on each side equals a number.

Have one child begin by rolling the die. Using the key the child chooses the body part that matches the number. Now it is the next person's turn. Play continues until the first person completes her entire robot.

You can also make it a cooperative game by having all children build the same robot.

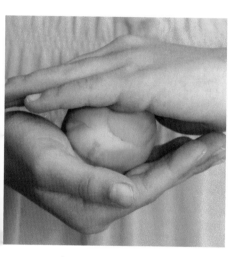

Little Blue and Little Yellow
By Leo Lionni

One day friends, Blue and Yellow, cannot find each other. Finally they discover each other and hug. But what has happened? Now they are green. Will their parents be able to figure out who they are?

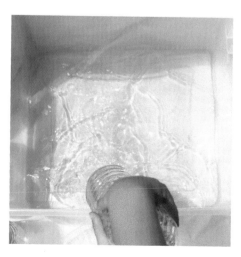

color mixing playdough

Chelsey Marashian, B.Ed – Buggy and Buddy

In this story two friends, Little Blue and Little Yellow, are so excited to see each other that they hug. This friendly hug causes them to mix and turn green. In this activity, kids will recreate this part of the story while exploring color mixing with play dough.

materials

blue playdough
yellow playdough
optional: red playdough

NOTE: homemade playdough recipe on page 107-108

After reading the story together, revisit the page where Little Blue and Little Yellow turn green. Talk about why this happened.

Give each child a small ball of yellow playdough and a small ball of blue playdough. Invite them to mix the two balls of playdough together using their hands. What happened?

Do this activity again using different ratios of yellow playdough to blue playdough. *How many different shades of green can you make?*

Optional: Do this same activity with red playdough. *What will happen if we mix red playdough with yellow playdough?* Red playdough with blue playdough?

Observe all the colors you created and use them for some fun sensory play when you're done.

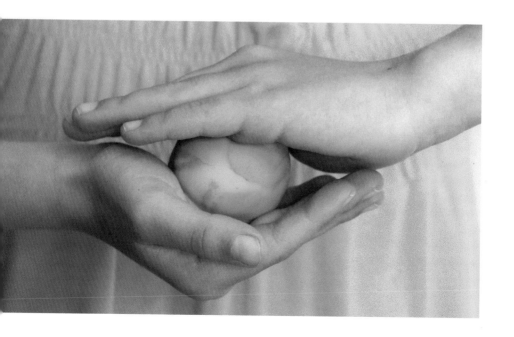

color changing flower

Meredith Magee Donnelly, MS, Ed – Homegrown Friends

The simple tale of two friends, little blue and little yellow, encompasses so many learning opportunities regarding friendship, emotions, family relations and, of course, color recognition and color mixing. This activity is a fun way to explore color mixing and science to create your own "Little Blue and Little Yellow" flower.

materials

white flower (rose, carnation, daisy)
2 cups, small vases or mason jars per 1 flower
yellow and blue food coloring or liquid watercolors
water
clear packing tape
knife or scissors

Begin by adding a couple of inches of water to 2 jars. Add a good deal of blue and yellow food coloring to the water, 1 color per jar.

Adult job: split the stem of the rose from the bottom to the top leaving the top inch of the flower stem alone. Position one part of the stem in the yellow water and one part of the stem in the blue water. Secure each part of the stem to the inside of the jar using clear packing tape. This will help keep the stems from breaking.

When a flower drinks, the water goes up from the bottom of the stem and travels to the top. After an hour we started to see the smallest amounts of blue traveling up half the petals and yellow up the other half. Within 10 hours the flower was a gorgeous half blue, half yellow.

Talk about how different parts of the stem are responsible for different flower petals. The part of the stem that was drinking the blue water was responsible for the blue petals and the part of the stem drinking the yellow water was taking care of the yellow flowers. We kept our flower out for about 4 days to observe.

Children can keep an observation journal throughout the process.

color mixing water play

Jaime Williams – Frogs, Snails and Puppy Dog Tails

Here is a fun hands-on, color mixing activity. My kids can never get enough water play at my house. This activity is a perfect excuse to get outside, but can also be done indoors too.

materials

empty plastic bottles
yellow and blue food coloring
water
water table or large plastic bin

Gather supplies for the color mixing activity before introducing the activity. Fill up a few bottles with water and add yellow or blue food coloring to the water bottles.

Discuss the colors and review the story of *Little Blue and Little Yellow*. Fill the bin with a little water. Do not add color to the water.

Children can explore by pouring the blue and yellow water bottles into the water bin. As the colors mix children will observe the water turning green.

Once all the water bottles are added to the water bin the children can continue to play. Water play is a fun and simple sensory play activity, and a great way to practice color mixing, pouring and scooping. This activity supports teamwork and sharing. Additional materials such as watering cans and bowls can be added. Great child led play!

friendship puffy paint

Colleen Beck, OTR/L – Sugar Aunts

This process art activity uses homemade puffy paint that combines to create a lovely work of art, inspired by the simple and beautiful blobs of color in *Little Blue and Little Yellow*. Splattering colors of paint on a paper and watching the puffy paint form is just part of the fun with this art activity. We discover through the mixture of blue and yellow paint that differences in color or appearance just don't matter. In the end, true friendship can see past differences in people and families.

materials

¼ cup flour
4 tablespoons warm water
blue and yellow food coloring
paint brushes

To make this homemade puffy paint, mix together the flour and water, stirring until all of the lumps of flour are thoroughly combined. Separate the flour/water mixture into two separate bowls. Add a few drops of blue food coloring to one bowl and add the yellow food coloring to the other bowl.

Using paint brushes, splatter the paint onto paper. Mix some of the blue and yellow paints together. Children can also paint details described in the narrative of the book.

When completed, place the paper into a microwave and cook for 30 seconds. The paints should puff up to create textured puffy paint.

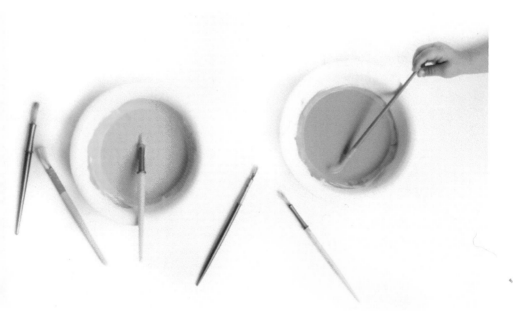

color mixing gel bags

Jen Kossowan, B.Ed – Mama.Papa.Bubba.

Little Blue and Little Yellow is such a classic children's story. As a teacher, I've used it year after year to introduce basic color theory to my students and it's been the jumping off point for many great hands-on color explorations. In this sensory-rich activity, children will explore how primary colors can be combined to make secondary colors, just as seen in the book.

materials

snack-sized zip-close bags
clear hair gel
food coloring in red, yellow, and blue
clear tape (if desired)

Fill three baggies with clear hair gel and use food coloring to tint one red, one blue, and one yellow. For extra security, seal all four sides of the bags with tape or double bag them placing the zip closures on opposite sides. Remove the excess air and zip each bag close, taping the top shut. Mix the food coloring into the gel by gently squishing the baggies until you have a uniform color.

On a white surface, overlap the blue and yellow baggies to explore color mixing. Flattened bags work best. Ask questions like *What do you see?* and *Why do you think this happens?* Next introduce the red baggie. Explore the three gel bags and pose questions such as *How many colors can we create?* and *Is there any way we can see all of the colors at once?*

The gel baggies last for weeks and make a great addition to a light table. For another fun twist, the bags can also be taped to a window that gets plenty of light.

Red
By Michael Hall

Red's name matches his exterior color, but that is not how he feels inside. He colors blue. Everyone around him tries to get him to color red, but nothing works. Red feels miserable. Finally, a new friend embraces who he truly is and helps him discover and and be proud of his true identity.

mixed-up taste test

Chelsey Marashian, B.Ed – Buggy and Buddy

Although Red crayon seems like he should color red because of his red paper wrapping, he always colors blue. He shows us we can't always judge a book by its cover. This science lesson helps drive home the message that things aren't always what they seem. Children will taste various drinks which aren't the color you'd expect them to be. We will see how all our senses work together to help us identify various flavors.

materials

variety of drinks: water, milk, apple juice, lemonade etc.
cups
food dye
Note: This activity can still be done without using food dye. Instead of disguising the drink with color, you can have your child shut his/her eyes when doing the taste test.

Be sure the children are out of the room for the setup of this lesson. Collect as many different drinks as you'd like to use in this activity. We used five: water, apple juice, lemonade, milk, and white grape juice. Pour a bit of each drink into its own cup. Add a few drops of different food coloring to each glass and stir. Now the drinks are not the color you'd expect them to be.

Invite the children into the room and tell them the five drinks they will be tasting. Their job is to guess which cup holds the correct drink, but there's a twist. Not only has the color of the drink changed, but the children will also not be able to use their sense of smell.

Invite the children to hold their noses and take a sip from each cup. *Which drink do you think is in each cup?* Now try it again without holding your nose. *Is it easier to guess?*

Your nose is actually more important than your eyes or tongue in determining the taste of foods and drinks.

crayon wrappers

Jen Kossowan, B.Ed – Mama.Papa.Bubba.

Red's message about accepting both yourself and others for who they really are is an important one. In this self-reflective art and literacy activity, children will have an opportunity to investigate what makes them who they are as individuals.

materials

crayon template
pencil
black marker
crayons
scissors

Begin by reading the book and exploring what it means to be true to your inner self. Invite the children to share things that make them who they truly are. In order to get past basic facts such as names, ages, and physical qualities, pose the question *What are some things that make you who you really are that people might not know?* This will encourage the children to dig deeper and think about their passions, dislikes, strengths, etc. Brainstorm a list of great adjectives to describe people (adventurous, brave, careful, polite, independent, patient, etc.) and invite the children to share which ones suit them.

Give children a copy of the crayon template and explain that they'll be using it to design a crayon wrapper that reflects the true them. Invite them to write their names in thick block letters where a color's name usually appears on a crayon wrapper.

Ask them to fill the crayon with words that reflect their individuality. Depending on the child, he or she can use invented spelling to write their words independently, or you can help them with the process. Once their name and describing words are written in pencil, invite them to trace them in black marker. The children can also add small illustrations for each of the ideas if they choose.

Afterwards, use crayons to color in the entire crayon, encouraging the children to use a color (or colors!) that they feel represent them as a person. Cut out the crayons and then display them for all to see.

75

crayon math game

Jaime Williams – Frogs, Snails and Puppy Dog Tails

Anytime crayons are involved you know the activity is going to be lots of fun. This crayon math game can be modified for different aged children. It can be a simple crayon counting game, basic addition learning or a game to work on adding and subtracting all within the same game. When the children saw the large bowl of fresh crayons come out, all of their eyes got big and I knew this was going to be a new favorite activity.

materials

crayons
bowl
index cards
markers

Prior to introducing the math game put four 24 count boxes of crayons into a medium sized bowl. Next, create the number cards for the game. Using white index cards write numbers 1-10 or the numbers you wish to work on. Using colorful markers write the numbers more than once so that there can be two of every number. Make cards with an addition sign, equal sign, and subtraction sign.

Now it is time to play. Set the bowl of crayons out as well as the cards. Have each child select a card and then count out how many crayons they need to make that number.

Older children can select two cards and put the addition card in between the two numbers and the equal card at the end so they can do simple addition equations. Do the same thing for subtraction equations. Children will have so much fun counting, adding and subtracting.

food predictions

Meredith Magee Donnelly, MS, Ed – Homegrown Friends

Just like how everyone around Red crayon made assumptions about him based on his outward appearance, children often see a food and declare *I don't like it* without even tasting it. This experiment challenges children to make predictions about how food tastes, what it is called and how it looks on the inside based solely on the how it looks on the outside.

materials

various vegetables and fruits- choose unusual ones that look different on the outside than they do on the inside
food prediction printable- one per food per child (page 139)
pencil

Purchase fruits and/or vegetables that are more unusual for your area and look different on the outside than they appear on the inside. The choices will largely depend on where you are living and the food the children usually eat. For this experiment we used jicama, pomegranate and a red banana.

Give each child food prediction sheets for each food and a pencil. Have children write their names at the top of the papers. Children will observe one food item at a time and predict what the name of the food is, what the food looks like on the inside and what the food tastes like. Children can write independently using inventive spelling or dictate the words.

After making predictions, open each food and observe. After you name each food have the children write the observation on their sheets. Next, the children can write or dictate how the food looks on the inside. Finally, have each child taste the food and record their observations.

Discuss the findings as a group. Pose questions such as *Were any of your predictions correct? Were any of your predictions incorrect? Who liked a food that they had never tried before?*

unique swoopy art

Colleen Beck, OTR/L – Sugar Aunts

This colorful and abstract process art is inspired by *Red*, a book about the mistaken identity of a blue crayon. The mislabeled crayon discovers his true self by following his own path. Colorful swirls, swoops, and circles make up this crayon art project. Children can create impressive artwork with many colors as they emulate *Red's* message of following one's own path, staying true to oneself, and following through with one's own style.

materials

crayons
loop rubber bands
paper

Use a loop rubber band to encircle 4-5 crayons. Add 2-3 more rubber bands to create a large "crayon".

Children can use their large crayons to create gross motor art with swoops and big arm motions as they combine colors. Try making this artwork on a large scale by using a roll of butcher paper. Add details with a black crayon, or fill in shapes with the multi-color crayon.

As the children are creating their artwork, use the book as a conversation starter to discuss qualities that make them special and that they are perfect just the way they are, much like their colorful artwork.

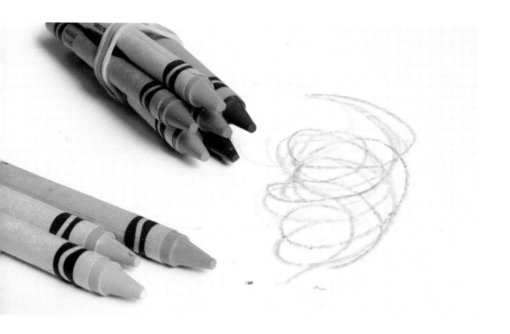

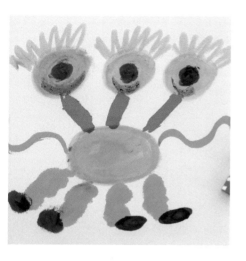

The Adventures of Beekle
By Dan Santat

In a magical land, an imaginary friend waits to be chosen by a child. When time passes and no one chooses him, he decides to go in search of his special friend.

playdough friends

Jen Kossowan, B.Ed – Mama.Papa.Bubba.

The Adventures of Beekle is a whimsical and magical story that invites children to be imaginative and creative, while giving them full permission to enjoy the company of an imaginary friend. In this creative sensory play activity, children will let their imaginations take over while creating and naming their very own 'Beekle'.

materials

playdough in several colors
googly eyes
buttons
acrylic gems
pipe cleaners
lollipop sticks
miniature crowns made from craft foam or thick card stock
divided tray

Before starting this activity with the children, put together your creation station by arranging your playdough and loose parts in the divided tray.

Begin by reading the book and exploring the concepts of imagination and imaginary friends. Pose questions such as *How can we use our imaginations?* and *How can imaginary friends be helpful?* Explain that you'll be using your imaginations and all sorts of fun craft items to create imaginary friends of your own.

Set out the creation station and invite the children to select some playdough to use as the base for their imaginary friends. Encourage them to use the loose parts as they please in order to form their playmates. The beauty of this is that the dough can be formed into any shape, and all of the materials can simply be pressed or stuck into it - no scissors or glue required!

Once their imaginary friends are complete, invite the children to share them. Ask questions such as *Does your imaginary friend have a name?* and *What makes him or her a good friend?* When finished, the play dough friends can be disassembled, the parts sorted, and the creation station stored for next time.

build a friend bin

Colleen Beck, OTR/L – Sugar Aunts

A sensory bin inspires creative play. This build-an-imaginary-friend sensory bin is based on Beekle and the other imaginary friends in *The Adventures of Beekle: The Unimaginary Friend*. Just like the island for imaginary friends, this sensory bin is full of colors, textures, and different items that will allow kids to build their own imaginary friends.

materials

large plastic bin
sensory bin filler- try dry beans, field corn, colored rice, small pebbles, or cotton balls
craft supplies- feathers, googly eyes, craft sticks, craft pom poms, and tissue paper
glue

The detailed and colorful illustrations of the book are depicted in a multi-textural sensory bin that provides children with a sensory play activity where they can find items to create their own imaginary friend.

Fill a plastic bin or water table with the sensory filler material. Hide craft supplies in the sensory filler.

Allow children to play and explore all of the textures as they find materials. Children can create and build an imaginary friend using items from the sensory bin. Once the imaginary friends are completed, use them in pretend play.

imaginary stick friends

Jaime Williams – Frogs, Snails and Puppy Dog Tails

Making your own imaginary craft stick puppets is a wonderful way to explore *The Adventures of Beekle* after story time. This is a simple and fun book activity that would be easy to do at home or in a classroom setting. Children can retell the story or make up their own versions.

materials

craft sticks
paint
paper
markers
glue

Set out the materials to make the imaginary stick friends. Begin by painting the craft sticks. Once dry, children can add details with markers and paper.

Children can create a friend from the book or use their imaginations to make new friends. To create Beekle, invite the children to add a yellow paper crown and permanent marker eyes and mouth to a white craft stick. If they would like to make something different allow them to use the materials freely in order to bring their vision to life.

The finished craft stick friends are perfect for imaginary play.

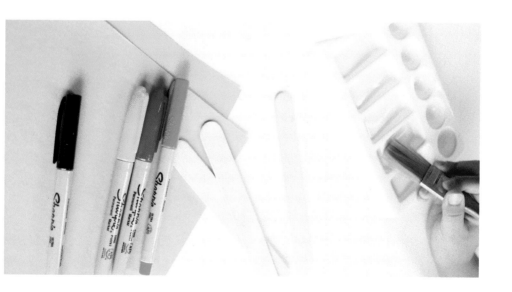

paper bag crowns

Chelsey Marashian, B.Ed – Buggy and Buddy

Both my children really relate to *The Adventures of Beekle*. Reading the story often initiates conversations about friendship and perseverance and always seems to inspire all kinds of pretend play. In this activity, kids will create their own crowns (just like Beekle's) using a paper bag. They can then use their finished crowns to role play meeting someone new and later for dramatic play.

materials

brown paper grocery bag
scissors
watercolor paints and paintbrush
stapler or tape
pom poms and sequins (optional)

Start by making your paper bag crown. You'll first need to cut a paper bag apart so you have one long piece of brown paper to work with. To do this, cut down one side of the paper bag and then around all four sides of the bottom.

Draw a crown shape on your paper and cut it out. Paint your crown with watercolor paints, and let it dry completely. You can leave it as it is or glue other decorations like pom poms or sequins onto your crown. Fit the crown around your child's head and staple or tape it to fit.

Discuss how Beekle and Alice felt when first meeting each other. *How did they become friends?* Talk about ways someone might introduce themself to a new friend and invite him or her to play.

Now it's time to role play meeting a new friend. Have your child wear his crown and act out how he would introduce himself to someone new he's just met. (They can role play with you or another child.) *What would you say? What expression might you have on your face? How would you and your new friend feel?*

When you're done, save your crown to inspire all kinds of imaginative play.

friend dice game

Meredith Magee Donnelly, MS, Ed – Homegrown Friends

Children will explore all that their minds can imagine with this fun friend dice game. With the help of a die, children will each create their own unique creature while also practicing counting and number recognition. Nothing is off limits. Whatever the mind can imagine is possible.

materials

dice (1 die per child or pair of children)
paper
crayons/markers/paint sticks/pencils

Begin by giving each child a piece of paper and access to drawing materials such as paint sticks, crayons, markers or colored pencils. Next tell the children that they will be drawing their own imaginary friends, but there's a catch. The die will be used to determine the number of body parts the friend will have.

Start with the head. Have each child pick the color he wants for his imaginary friend's head. Next each child rolls her die to determine the number of heads to draw. After the children draw the heads, move on to the neck. Follow the same steps for all body parts.

When children are finished with their drawings, than can name their new imaginary friends.

Chrysanthemum
By Kevin Henkes

Chrysanthemum loves her name until she goes to school and some classmates start making fun of her. Suddenly, Chrysanthemum's self-esteem wilts until she meets a teacher who challenges the bullying and helps Chrysanthemum's confidence.

character trait necklaces

Colleen Beck, OTR/L – Sugar Aunts

With this character traits necklace craft, children will explore the qualities that make them who they are. Just like Chrysanthemum did, they will learn that it is their unique qualities that make them special rather than their names. Children can discover how original they are and that no other flower necklace craft will be exactly like their own.

materials

cupcake liners in a variety of colors
scissors
glue
marker
string or plastic lacing thread
tape

Using the scissors, cut into the cupcake liners toward the center to create petal like shapes. Cut other cupcake liners around the center fold to create a circle.

With the marker, write or allow children to dictate qualities about themselves that make them special.

Glue the circles onto different colored petal cupcake liners. Tape the flowers onto the plastic lacing thread or string. While making the craft, discuss how every child is unique and special and that their qualities are what make them who they really are.

salt writing tray

Jaime Williams – Frogs, Snails and Puppy Dog Tails

Nothing like finding a book with a title you just cannot help but say over and over again. It may take the children a few tries, but I'm guessing they will be saying Chrysanthemum over and over once they get it. Since this book is all about names, it is perfect to pair it with a name activity. A salt writing tray allows children to practice writing their names in a unique and fun way.

materials

tray
colored paper
salt
marker
paint brushes and unsharpened pencils (optional)

Line a tray with colored paper. Pour the salt over the paper. Add just enough salt to cover the paper. Less salt makes it easier for children to write with their finger on the tray. Paint brushes or unsharpened pencils can be used as well.

Next, use the remaining colored paper to cut up several cards. Using a marker, write the letters of the children's names and mix up the letters.

Giving them the stack of cards, invite the children to search for the letters needed to create their names. When the letters have been found, the children can use them as a guide when writing their names in the salt tray.

This inexpensive activity is easy to set up for either a home or classroom environment and is perfect for working on pre-writing skills and name recognition.

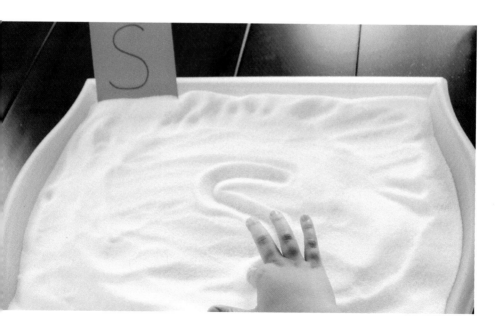

friendship flowers

Chelsey Marashian, B.Ed – Buggy and Buddy

When I was a classroom teacher, *Chrysanthemum* was one of the stories we read often, especially at times throughout the year when we needed to discuss any issues with teasing or what to do if someone is hurting your feelings. We would talk about what makes a good friend and how to be a good friend to others. This activity builds on that important theme of friendship. Children will create flowers and brainstorm descriptive words that describe good friends.

materials

small paper plate
construction paper or cardstock
scissors
marker
glue
paint (optional)

Start with your small paper plate. This will be the center of your flower. You can leave it as is, or paint it. My kids enjoyed painting it with a few colors and swirling them right on the plate.

Cut some strips of colored construction paper or cardstock to serve as your flower petals. Brainstorm words that describe the characteristics of a good friend. Invite your child to write one descriptive word onto each petal. You can have younger children dictate the words to you as you write the words. Glue each petal around the outside of your paper plate. Add a stem and leaves if you'd like.

If you're interested in extending this activity, have children draw pictures of themselves with a good friend or being a good friend and glue them onto the center of the paper plate flower.

Hang up your finished artwork. Not only will the paper plate flowers brighten any room, but they'll serve as great reminders of the importance of being a good friend.

personalized name art

Jen Kossowan, B.Ed – Mama.Papa.Bubba.

Chrysanthemum is a classic book and a fabulous tool when teaching little ones about kindness, individuality, and being proud of who you are. In this activity, children will explore all of the ways they are special and create a beautiful piece of name art to showcase their individuality.

materials

white paper
permanent black markers, one thin and one thick
pencil
scissors, crayons, watercolor paint
paintbrushes
poster board
glue stick

Discuss how all names are special because they've been picked out especially for you. Invite the children to share some of the ways they are unique, encouraging them to think about their families, likes, strengths, accomplishments, and special features.

Depending on the children's ages, either have them write out their names in big, bold block letters, or provide the letters for them. Outline the letters in thick black permanent marker.

Invite the children to fill the letters of their names with drawings and words that show the many ways they're unique. They might include drawings of their families, their favorite sports, or what they like to eat, and they might write their middle names, their ages, or the names of their hometowns. Anything goes here, so long as it is about them!

When their pencil drawings are complete, ask the children to trace their drawings using thin permanent markers to really make them pop. The children can then color in their drawings using wax crayons before gently brushing on a coat of watercolor paint on top. Of course the wax will resist the paint and the completed letters will be beautifully colored!

As a final step, cut out the letters and mount them on a strip of poster board using a glue stick.

name hunt exploration

Meredith Magee Donnelly, MS, Ed – Homegrown Friends

Let's face it, children are sitting way too much during the day. That's why it is so important to create learning opportunities that get children up and moving. Scavenger hunts are one of the best ways to combine gross motor development and literacy. This name hunt exploration has children running, promotes teamwork, supports counting and explores letter and name recognition.

materials

colored construction paper
marker
scissors

Prior to introducing the scavenger hunt, write the letters of each child's name on small square pieces of construction paper. Choose a different color paper for each child to make the names easier to find and graph later. Next, hide the paper squares. This is a great opportunity to get kids outside. If you have playground equipment hide some of the squares on it so children have to use all different types of movement to find them.

Introduce the game by telling the children their names are hidden all around. Give each child the color they are looking for. Ready, set, go!

Once children find all the letters in their names it is time to graph them. You can do this on the ground, or use a glue stick and glue them on a large piece of paper to make a wall graph.

Once the names are graphed, count the letters in each name. Pose questions such as *Whose name has the most letters? How many children have 5 letters? Whose name has the least amount of letters? How many people's names start with M?*

Whoever You Are
By Mem Fox

Mem Fox takes readers on a gorgeous journey throughout the world. Each page is a celebration of diversity and an acknowledgment of our similarities as human beings.

multicultural playdough

Meredith Magee Donnelly, MS, Ed – Homegrown Friends

Embracing and celebrating our differences is at the heart of a great early childhood education. This multicultural playdough is a wonderful way to explore skin colors in a playful, age-appropriate way. Children can help make the initial playdough colors and then blend them together to make their unique skin color as well as their friends' skin colors too.

materials

2 cups flour
2 cups water
1 cup salt
4 teaspoons cream of tartar
2 tablespoons oil
food coloring- yellow, brown, black
playdough tools: rolling pins, people cookie cutters, googly eyes, pipe cleaners, etc.

Begin by making the playdough. Making playdough teaches children about measurement, following verbal and written instructions and scientific experimentation. Mix the flour, water, salt, cream of tartar and oil. Separate into 4 equal parts. We made 4 different skin colors beginning with a very pale cream, a light brown, a medium brown and very dark blackish-brown. After making each color heat in a pot on the stove stirring constantly until a ball forms. Place on a counter to cool. Do this process with each color.

Set out the playdough colors with a variety of playdough tools such as rolling pins, people cookie cutters, heart cutters, googly eyes and pipe cleaners. There is no right or wrong way to use the playdough.

Children can mix the colors kneading it with their hands to create their own skin colors. This is a great exercise to demonstrate through play that there are endless amounts of skin colors in the world. All of us are just different hues made up of the same parts. If interested children can name the skin colors they create. This is always fun.

inside & out portraits

Jen Kossowan, B.Ed – Mama.Papa.Bubba.

Mem Fox's message in *Whoever You Are* is clear - despite our many physical and circumstantial differences, on the inside, people are inherently similar. In this art activity, children will have the opportunity to showcase their individuality while celebrating the similarities that unite us as people.

materials

body template (2 copies per child)
pencil
crayons, pencil crayons, or markers
scissors
clear tape
mirror (optional, but recommended)

Discuss the idea that although people around the world have many differences, they also have many things in common. Brainstorm several ways people are different (their skin colors, homes, schools, languages, countries, etc.) and several ways they are often the same (their smiles, joys, hurts, hearts, blood, etc.)

Using a copy of the body template, invite the children to draw what they look like on the outside. Encourage them to include their defining features (glasses, freckles, the way their hair is styled, the clothing they enjoy wearing, etc.) so that the portrait truly looks like them. Use mirrors to help add details along the way.

Next, talk about what the inside of our bodies look like. Ask the children to tell you a little bit about what is found underneath our skin (bones, a heart, lungs, a stomach, blood, etc.) Give the children another copy of the body template, this time inviting them to draw the insides of their bodies (what's important here are the elements, not the placement).

Invite the children to color both the inside and outside portraits before carefully cutting them out. Attach the portraits with a small piece of clear tape along the top of the head so that it can fold open and shut. Invite the children to share their portraits, reiterating the fact that though we're all different on the outside, our insides are the same.

make a thaumatrope

Chelsey Marashian, B.Ed – Buggy and Buddy

To help illustrate the lesson that throughout the world we share the same hopes and dreams, children will create a popular, old fashioned toy called a thaumatrope. A thaumatrope is a circular disk with two separate pictures on each side attached to a string. When the string is twirled and un-twirled quickly, the two pictures appear to combine into one.

materials

paper plate (or posterboard)
scissors
glue
single hole punch
yarn
markers, crayons, or colored pencils

Children will draw a picture related to the story onto each side of their thaumatrope. As the toy is spun, the two pictures will combine into one, showing that no matter where we are, we are all part of the same world and share the same hopes and dreams.

Cut out a circle with about a 3-inch diameter from your paper plate or posterboard. Use your hole punch to punch out two holes directly across from each other.

Use your markers or crayons to color a picture onto each side of your circle. Think about things related to the story that make sense when combined. We drew the Earth on one side and hearts on the other. When the pictures combined it represented our love spreading over the whole world! (If the markers are going through your posterboard or paper plate, draw your pictures onto two separate circles and then glue them together.)

Once you are done drawing your pictures, cut two long pieces of yarn. Tie one piece through each hole in your circle.

To play with your thaumatrope, grab each piece of yarn and hold them out to the side. Twirl the yarn and watch it un-twirl. As the pictures spin, they'll appear to combine.

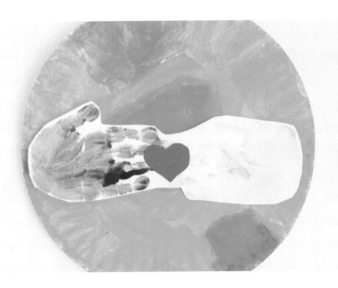

handprint world craft

Jaime Williams – Frogs, Snails and Puppy Dog Tails

My children can never get enough book crafts. This cute handprint craft is a wonderful extension activity. After reading *Whoever You Are,* get your simple craft materials out while enjoying making your own piece of art.

materials

paper plate
white cardstock
brown, cream, blue, and green paint
red construction paper
paint brush
glue

Choose paints representing different skin tones. Paint the children's hands with the skin-toned paints and create handprints on white cardstock paper. Let the prints dry.

Using blue and green paints create the earth on the paper plate and let dry. Cut out hearts from red paper.

Once the paint dries cut out the handprints from the paper. Glue the handprints on the paper plate world. Glue a red paper heart in the middle of the hands.

diversity collages

Colleen Beck, OTR/L – Sugar Aunts

This collaborative art project celebrates the diversity, similarities, and differences that are reflected in *Whoever You Are*. The colorful and detailed illustrations inspire details in this joint artwork. Children will realize the joy of a group project as they work with peers using pieces that come from many sources to create a complex composition.

materials

large variety of small items: craft supplies, recycled items, scrap material, etc.
glue
cardboard box

Prior to creating this artwork, ask children to gather supplies from home or around the classroom. Add all of the parts together in a large bin.

Children can create together, adding glue and pieces of the project in a peer activity. As the children create, talk about how the parts of this artwork have come from many different places and are various colors, textures, and sizes.

Discuss how parts of the creation are alike and different, and just like each of us, together all of the items create a unique and beautiful collage.

Penguin and Pinecone
By Salina Yoon

Penguin loves his new friend Pinecone, but soon learns that Pinecone needs to live in a warm forest. Penguin returns Pinecone to his home.
Returning much later, Penguin discovers that Pinecone has grown into a large tree, but their love remains the same.

pinecone exploration

Chelsey Marashian, B.Ed – Buggy and Buddy

One of the most surprising events in the story *Penguin and Pinecone* is when Penguin goes to visit his friend Pinecone after some time and realizes he's grown into... a large tree! This unexpected part of the story provides a wonderful opportunity for children to learn more about pinecones through observation and exploration. In this activity, we'll be setting up a pinecone exploration center complete with all kinds of materials to spark curiosity in your little learner.

materials

pinecones
optional: other tree seeds like acorns, maple seeds, seed pods etc.
blank paper
crayons
magnifying glass
measuring tape

Start by taking a nature walk with your child. Keep your eyes open for pinecones (and any other tree seeds you come across). Gather them and bring them home to explore.

Select an area of your home or classroom that's easily accessible to children, like a kids' table or tray. Place your pinecones and other tree seeds onto the exploration area. Add other items to the exploration center that will help encourage all kinds of sensory exploration.

We added a magnifying glass to see details of our pinecones up close, some blank paper and crayons to encourage journaling, drawing, and labeling, and some measuring tape to compare the sizes of our pinecones. You could also check out some books about pinecones from your local library and add those to the center.

Leave the exploration center out for a few days so your children can go back and explore at their leisure. When you are finished with your exploration center, save your pinecones. You can decorate them with craft materials like pom poms and yarn or use them for retelling the story.

fork painted pine trees

Jaime Williams – Frogs, Snails and Puppy Dog Tails

Here is a fun craft to do after reading *Penguin and Pinecone*. A few simple materials make this the perfect activity for home or school. The children love the opportunity to get out the paint!

materials

green paint
white cardstock paper
plastic forks
colored construction paper
scissors
glue
marker

Begin by putting green paint on a plate. Demonstrate how to dip the fork in the green paint and make the top of the pine tree on the paper. Cardstock paper works best because it is thicker than construction paper, but construction paper can also be used. Talk to the children about how to create the fork imprints to create a tree shape.

Dip the fork in green paint and begin making the top of the tree. Help guide children to use the fork prints to make a pine tree shape.

Once the paintings are dry add the finishing touches to the pine tree craft. Cut out trunks from the brown construction paper and glue them to the bottom of the tree.

Cut out strips of paper to make a scarf. Glue down one piece across the tree and one down. Add scarf details with black sharpie marker. Hang the new wall art and enjoy.

story retelling basket

Jen Kossowan, B.Ed – Mama.Papa.Bubba.

Penguin and Pinecone begs to be read again and again, and is perfect for retelling. In this hands-on literacy activity, children will use simple props to explore friendship and storytelling with Penguin and Pinecone being their jumping off point.

materials

basket
penguin figurine
small pinecones
tree figurines
pebbles
small colorful scarves cut from felt
large felt swatches in brown and white

Begin by reading the book and discussing its elements afterwards. Pose questions such as *Who are the characters in the story?*, *What settings does the story include?*, and *What is the story's main problem?* to guide the conversation. Invite the children to retell the story in their own words.

Introduce the basket of storytelling props and let the children explore the items. Discuss which elements of *Penguin and Pinecone* are represented by the included items. Invite the children to retell the story using the story retelling basket, encouraging them to take creative liberties and use the items as they see fit.

When finished, store the story retelling basket with your copy of *Penguin and Pinecone* for future storytelling opportunities.

growing love grass

Colleen Beck, OTR/L – Sugar Aunts

The sweet and simple story of Penguin's love for Pinecone inspires this growing plant science project. Grass growing through a heart made of orange yarn reminds us that "when you give love, it grows". The simple act of caring for planted grass seeds can bring the story to life as children water and care for their seeds.

materials

ceramic pot
paint
paint brush
soil
spoons (for scooping soil)
grass seed
orange yarn

Before planting the grass seed children can decorate their plant container with paint. Allow the pots to dry and then begin the planting activity.

Fill the pot ¾ full and sprinkle grass seeds into the soil. Add a few more scoops of soil to cover the seeds. Then, cut a small piece of orange yarn and place it in a heart shape over the seeds.

Water and place the seeds in a sunny spot as grass (and love) grow. Children can discuss the ways they can care for their plant and how they care for those they love.

pinecone print cards

Meredith Magee Donnelly, MS, Ed – Homegrown Friends

Just like Pinecone and Penguin, children have people in their lives that they love, but live far away. With this activity children will create gorgeous pinecone printed paper to use as notecards. Each child will choose a loved one to mail a happy card to.

materials

pinecones- you can find them in nature or at a craft store
long white paper- roll of butcher paper works well
variety of tempera paint colors
paper plates
markers/pens/pencil
envelopes

Roll out a large piece of paper. Squeeze the tempera paint onto each paper plate. Put out enough pine cones so that each child has at least one.

Children can dip their pinecones in the paint and then create prints on the paper. Give children the time and space to experiment with the different ways the pinecones can be used. Pose questions such as *What does it look like when you roll the pinecone on the paper? Does the top of the pinecone make a different print than the bottom of the pinecone?*

Once the children are done making prints let the paper dry. Next, cut the paper into notecards.

Each child chooses a loved one to write to. Children can write their own words or dictate the words and have an adult write. Put each card in an envelope and add the address and a stamp.

This would be a great opportunity to take a trip to the post office to mail the letters.

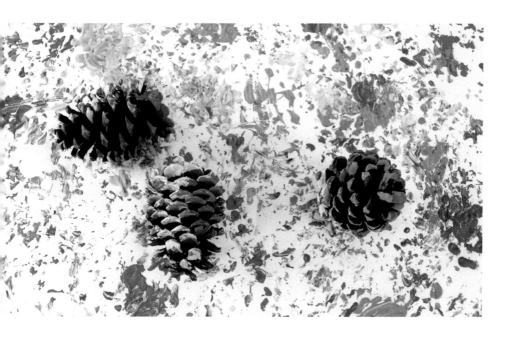

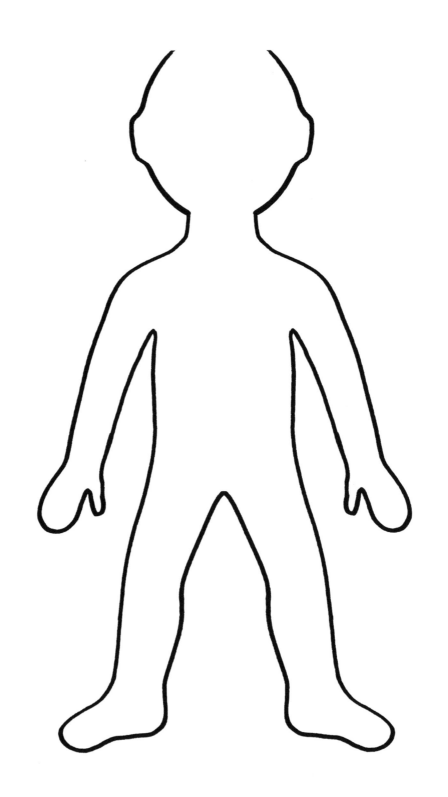

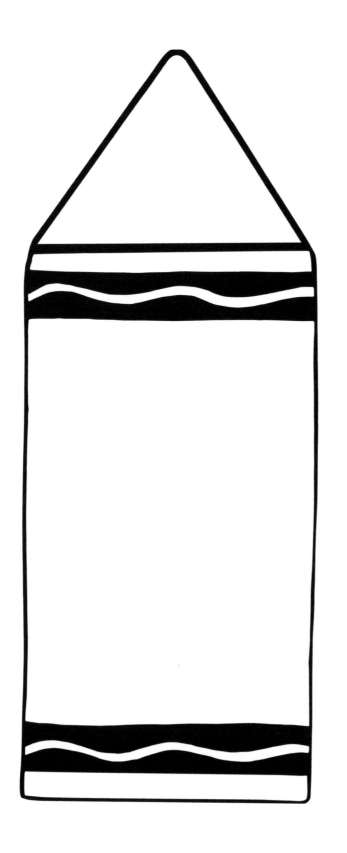

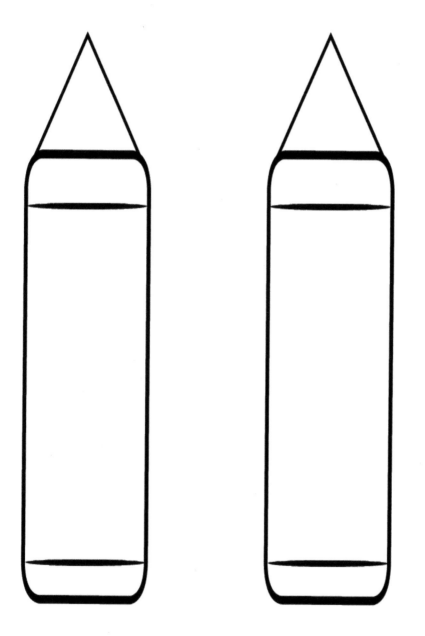

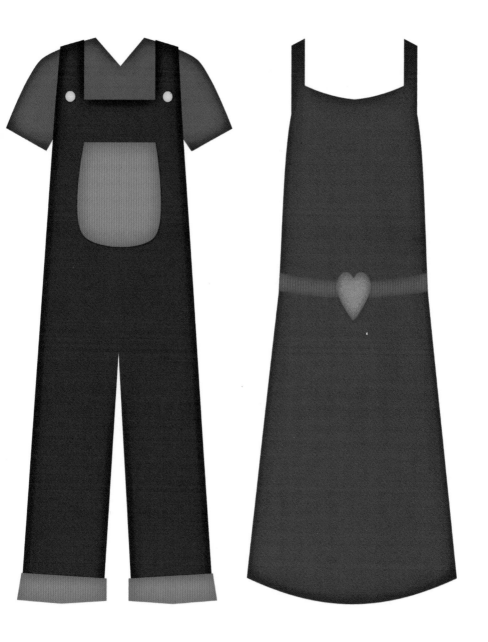

Dear _____Crayon,

Thank you for being my favorite crayon.

I love you because _____

_____.

My favorite thing to draw with you is

_____.

Have a great day!

_____

ROLL A ROBOT GAME

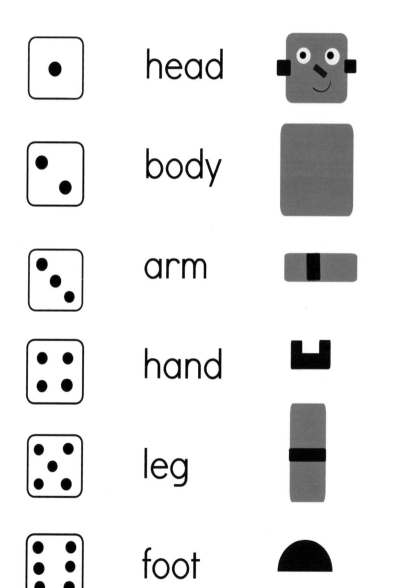

head

body

arm

hand

leg

foot

NAME: _____

Food Predictions Activity

NAME OF FOOD	PREDICTION	OBSERVATION
WHAT FOOD LOOKS LIKE ON THE INSIDE		
HOW FOOD TASTES		

Colleen Beck is a mom to four kids and an Occupational Therapist. She blogs at sugaraunts.com where she shares kids' activities and crafts designed to promote healthy, childhood development.

Jen Kossowan is a primary teacher turned stay-at home-mama to a spirited 5 year old and a sweet preemie babe. She blogs at Mama.Papa.Bubba. and can regularly be found sharing kids' activities and fun recipes on CBC Parents. Jen loves to travel, create recipes, take photos, and go on adventures around her hometown of Vancouver, British Columbia.

Meredith Magee Donnelly is an Early Childhoo Educator (MS, Ed), blogger at Homegrown Friends an mother of three children. Meredith was a Kindergarter teacher in NYC and now teaches toddler and prescho classes at her own studio. She resides with her childre and husband in West Hartford, CT.

Chelsey Marashian is a former elementary teacher of 13 years and is currently teaching enrichment classes for primary students at her neighborhood school, as well as blogging at Buggy and Buddy. She loves spending time with her two kids, husband, and puppy in sunny California.

Jaime Williams is a stay at home mom of three boys and blogger at Frogs and Snails and Puppy Dog Tail. With three boys, life never slows down, but she wouldn't have it any other way! She lives with her husband and children in Georgia.